AF605665
N
W
E
S
QLD
QUEENSLAND
SA
SOUTH
AUSTRALIA
NSW
NEW SOUTH WALES
ACT
AUSTRALIAN
CAPITAL
TERRITORY
VIC
VICTORIA
TAS
TASMANIA

KYLE SURRY
KIDS' GUIDE TO AUSTRALIA'S STATES & TERRITORIES
DISCOVERING
WESTERN AUSTRALIA
WA
REDBACK publishing

First Published 2026 by
Redback Publishing
Suite 6, 13a Narabang Way,
Belrose NSW 2085
Australia

www.redbackpublishing.com
orders@redbackpublishing.com

ISBN 978-1-761400-67-4

Author: Kyle Surry
Editors: Lucinda Dodds and Emma Dobinson
Designer: Redback Publishing

Original illustrations © Redback Publishing 2026
Originated by Redback Publishing

MIX
Paper from responsible sources
FSC
www.fsc.org
FSC™ C001507

Acknowledgements
Abbreviations: l—left, r—right, b—bottom, t—top, c—centre, m—middle
We would like to thank the following for permission to reproduce photographs: (Images © shutterstock, Alamy) p6-7 - Johannes van Keulen - Het Eyland Amsterdam, held at the National Library of Australia, Public Domain, https://commons.wikimedia.org/w/index.php?curid=17870436, p7t - George Pitt Morison - http://foundingdocs.gov.au/resources/picturealbum/i_wa1_72_1829b.jpg, Public Domain, https://commons.wikimedia.org/w/index.php?curid=18168401, p16 - GagliardiPhotography / Shutterstock.com, p18 - mikecphoto / Shutterstock.com, p23br - Ian Geraint Jones / Shutterstock.com, p27br - EQRoy / Shutterstock.com, p29ml - Squiresy92 including elements from Sodacan and User:Philtro - Own work, CC BY-SA 4.0, https://commons.wikimedia.org/w/index.php?curid=47261439

NATIONAL LIBRARY OF AUSTRALIA
A catalogue record for this book is available from the National Library of Australia

CONTENTS

Purnululu National Park

A LONG TIME AGO

Who Was There First?

Indigenous Australians have lived in Western Australia for at least 50,000 years. The Burrup Peninsula on the coast of Western Australia has thousands of places where there is ancient rock art. Burringurrah (Mount Augustus) is a huge single stone. It is twice as big as Uluru. Burringurrah is on Wadjari land, in the Gascoyne region.

Perth is located on the traditional lands of the Noongar people. Further north in the Kimberley area, the rock art and culture have histories that go back for thousands of years.

Cave paintings in the Kimberley

The Swan River was created by the serpent Waugal. The river's Indigenous name is Derbarl Yerrigan.

COLONY OF BRITAIN

Western Australia is the only state of Australia that was never included as part of the first settlement in New South Wales in 1788. Western Australia first became a colony of Britain in 1826, when a settlement was built at Albany.

In 1829, British settlers sailed all the way to the Swan River Settlement. This became the site of Perth.

In 1879, Alexander Forrest explored the Kimberley region and realised it was perfect for cattle raising. This was the start of the cattle industry in the north of Western Australia.

During the Gold Rush of the 1890s, people from overseas and from the other Australian colonies travelled to Western Australia to search for gold.

WHERE IS WESTERN AUSTRALIA?

WA covers about one third of Australia.

Western Australia is the largest state of Australia. Its shortened name is written as WA. Perth on the Swan River is the capital city. A very long land border separates WA from the rest of Australia.

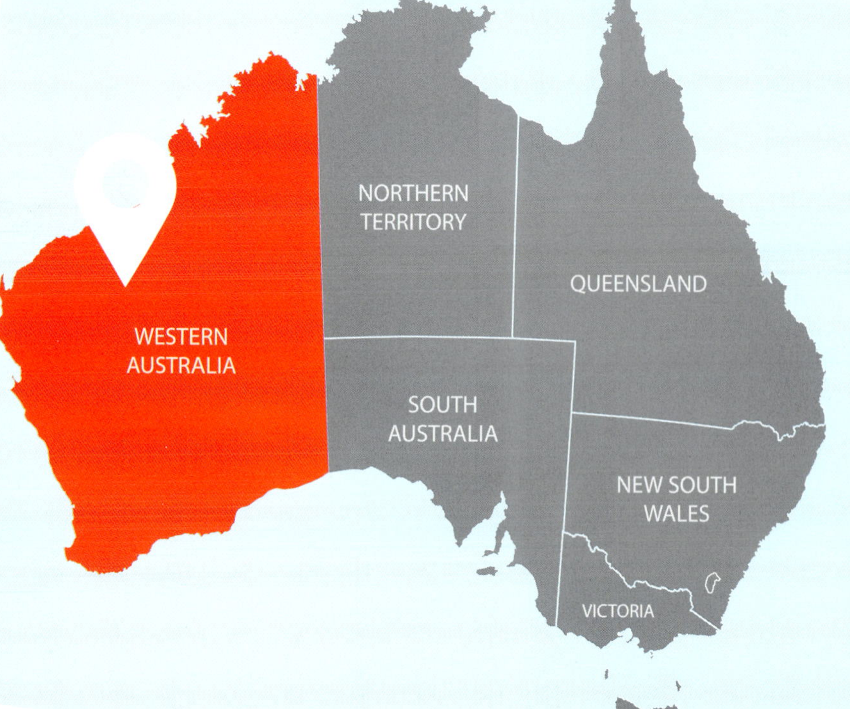

Where are the borders of Western Australia?

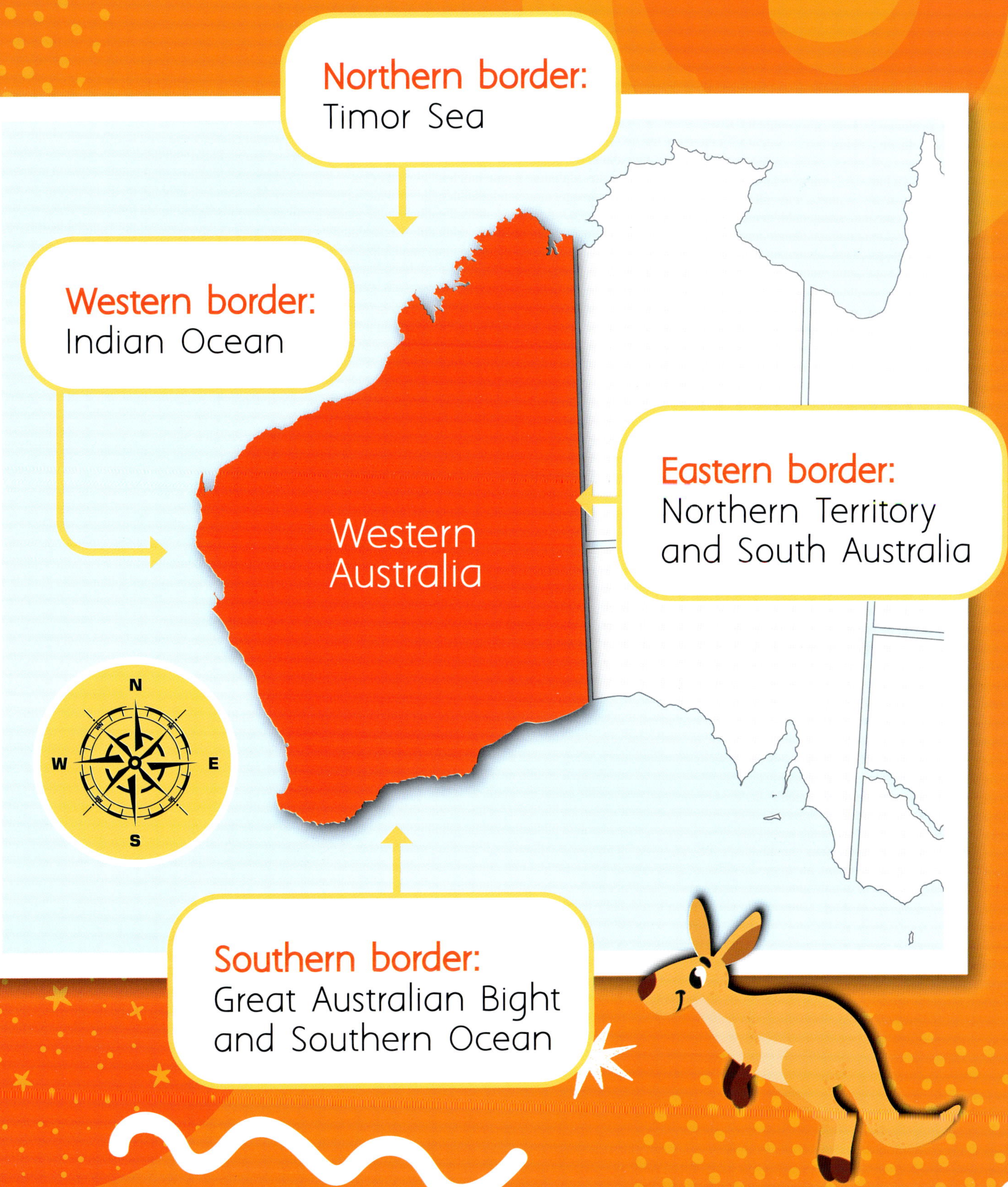

HOW MANY PEOPLE?

There are about three million people living in WA. Most of them live in or near Perth. There are very few people in the rest of the state.

About one out of every three people in WA was born overseas. The top three overseas countries they came from are England, New Zealand and India.

(ABS 2021)

ANCIENT LANDSCAPES

Gascoyne Region

In the west of WA, along the coast, are the tourist and wildlife sites of Shark Bay and Ningaloo Reef.

Goldfields-Esperance Region

In the 1800s, the Gold Rush brought thousands of miners to Kalgoorlie and Murchison in the southeast of WA.

Kimberley Region

In the far north of WA, the Kimberley has high rainfall and high temperatures.

Pilbara Region

In the northwest of WA, mining is important. It is a region of dry, red plains.

Mid-west Region

This region has the oldest rocks in the world, dating from four billion years ago.

Nullarbor Plain

The Nullarbor Plain begins near Kalgoorlie and extends into South Australia.

WORLD HERITAGE SITES

Shark Bay

In Hamelin Pool are the remains of an ancient life form that existed on Earth millions of years ago. They are called stromatolites.

Ningaloo Reef

This coral reef attracts dolphins, dugongs and whales.

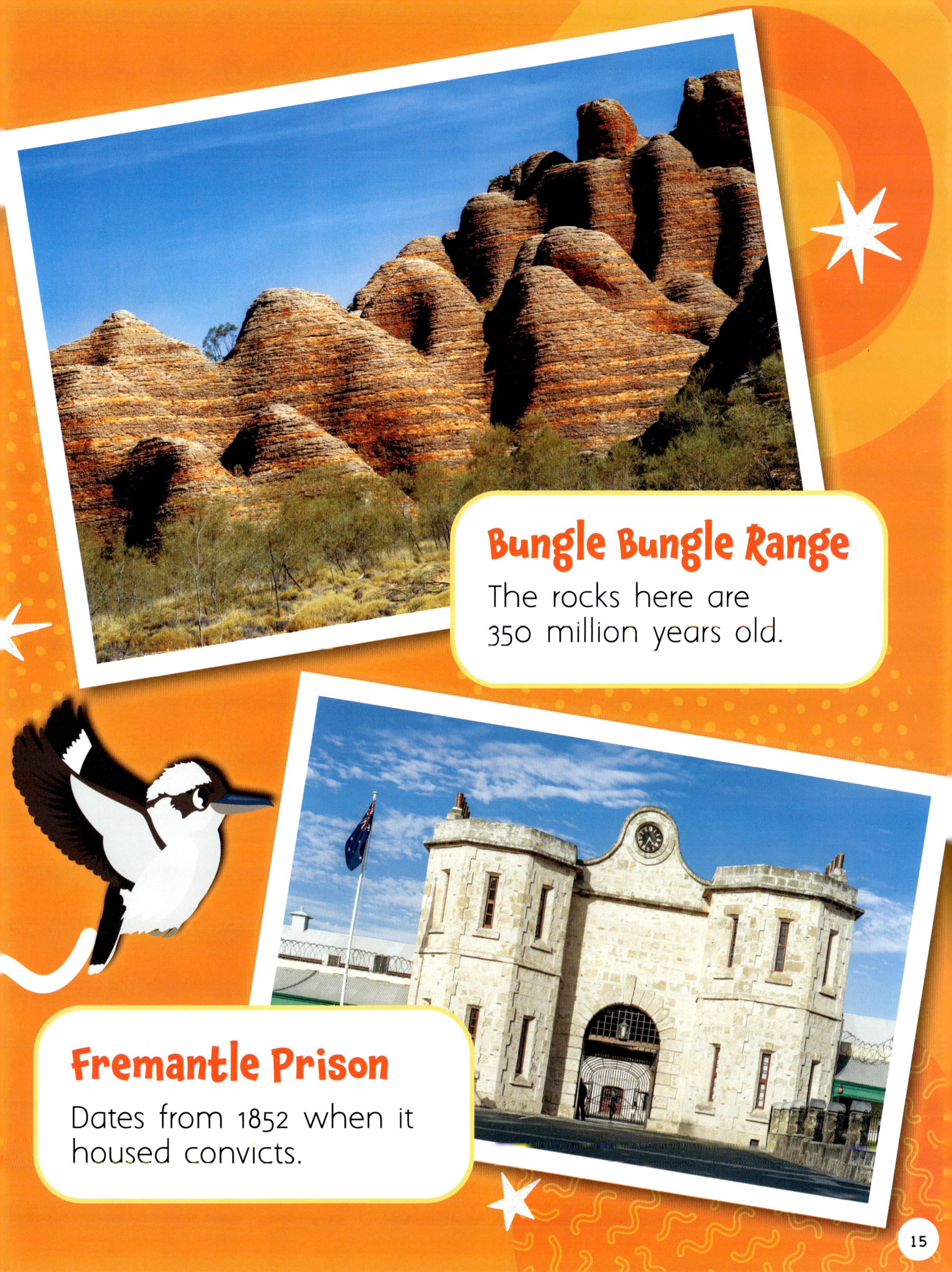

Bungle Bungle Range

The rocks here are 350 million years old.

Fremantle Prison

Dates from 1852 when it housed convicts.

THE BIGGEST CITIES

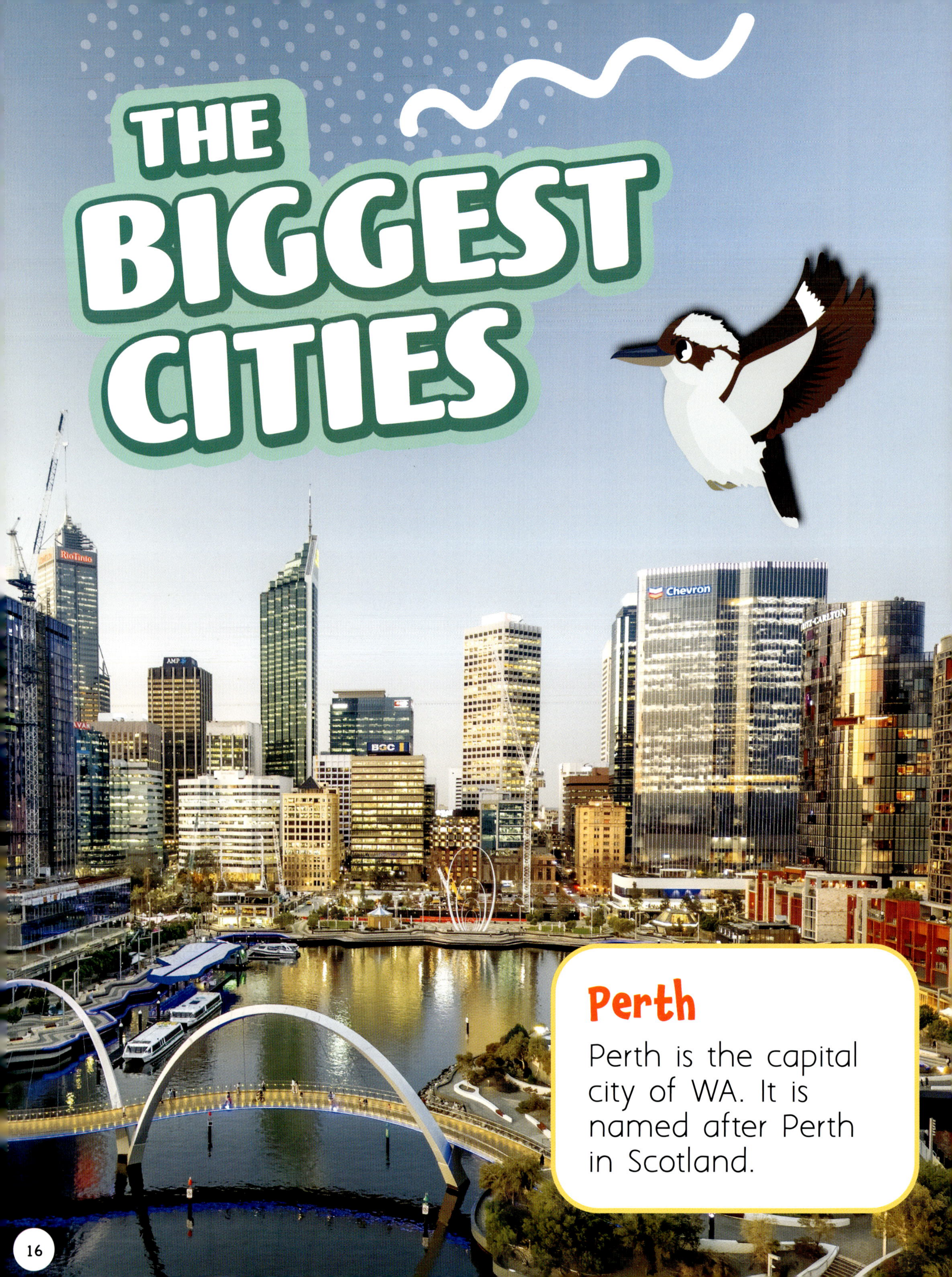

Perth

Perth is the capital city of WA. It is named after Perth in Scotland.

Bunbury

The Noongar name for this area is Goomburrup.

Albany

Albany was where the British decided to create a settlement for convicts in 1826.

Geraldton

Geraldton is on the coast. Produce from surrounding industries is exported through Geraldton Port.

Kalgoorlie

Gold mining began in Kalgoorlie in 1893, and it is still an important local industry.

ISLANDS OF WESTERN AUSTRALIA

- Rottnest Island
- Barrow Island
- Dirk Hartog Island
- Houtman Abrolhos Islands
- Monte Bello Islands
- Recherche Archipelago

DESERTS OF WESTERN AUSTRALIA

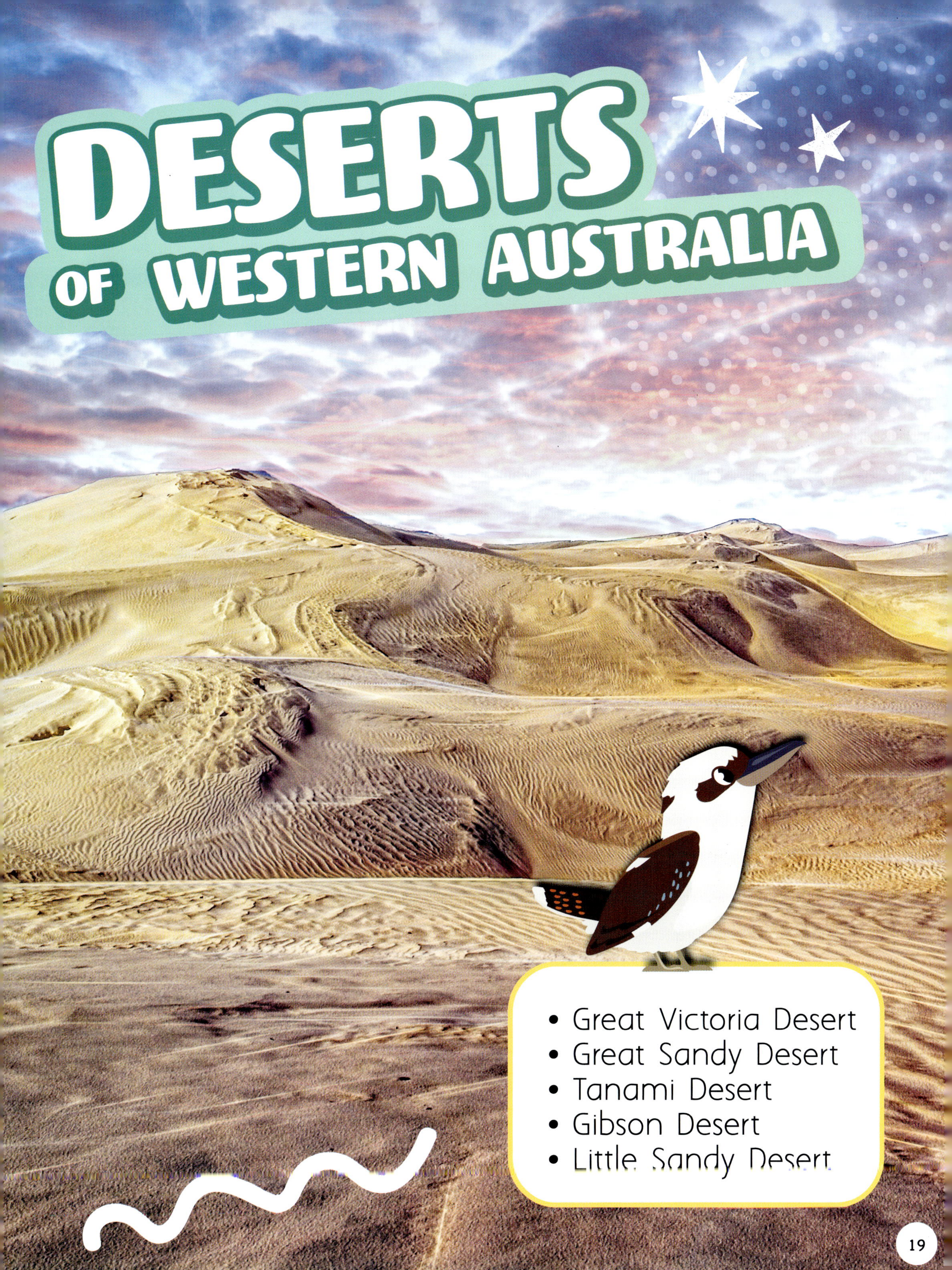

- Great Victoria Desert
- Great Sandy Desert
- Tanami Desert
- Gibson Desert
- Little Sandy Desert

MINING IN WESTERN AUSTRALIA

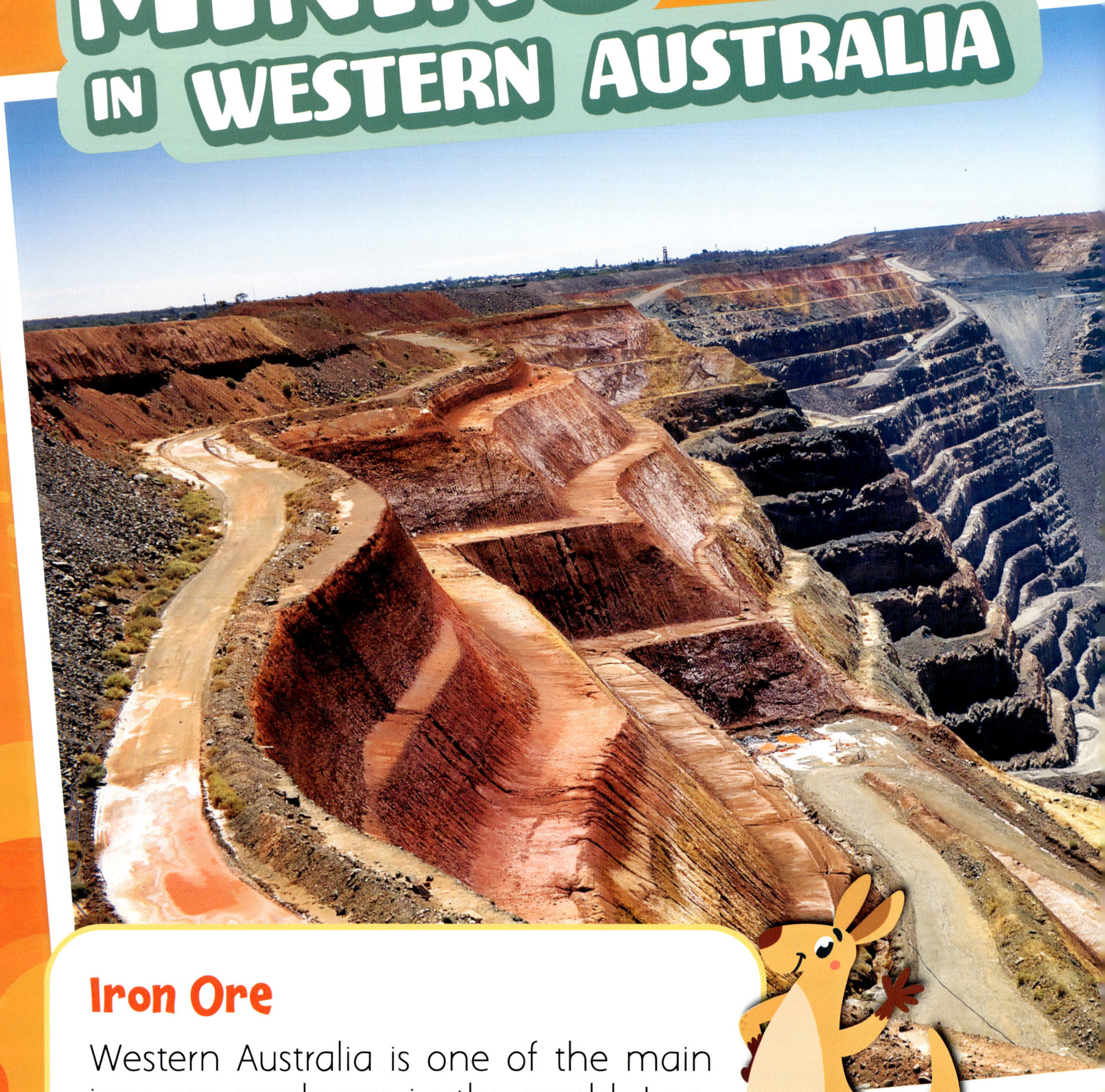

Iron Ore

Western Australia is one of the main iron ore producers in the world. Iron is needed to make steel.

Uranium

Uranium is used as fuel for nuclear power stations, for weapons and in medical testing. Uranium has been found in WA, but it has not yet been mined.

Lithium

Lithium from WA can be used to make batteries for electric cars, mobile phones and laptop computers.

Oil and Gas

WA mines oil and natural gas.

Gold

WA is the source of most of Australia's gold production.

Nickel

The main nickel mining in Australia is in WA.

CATTLE AND SHEEP

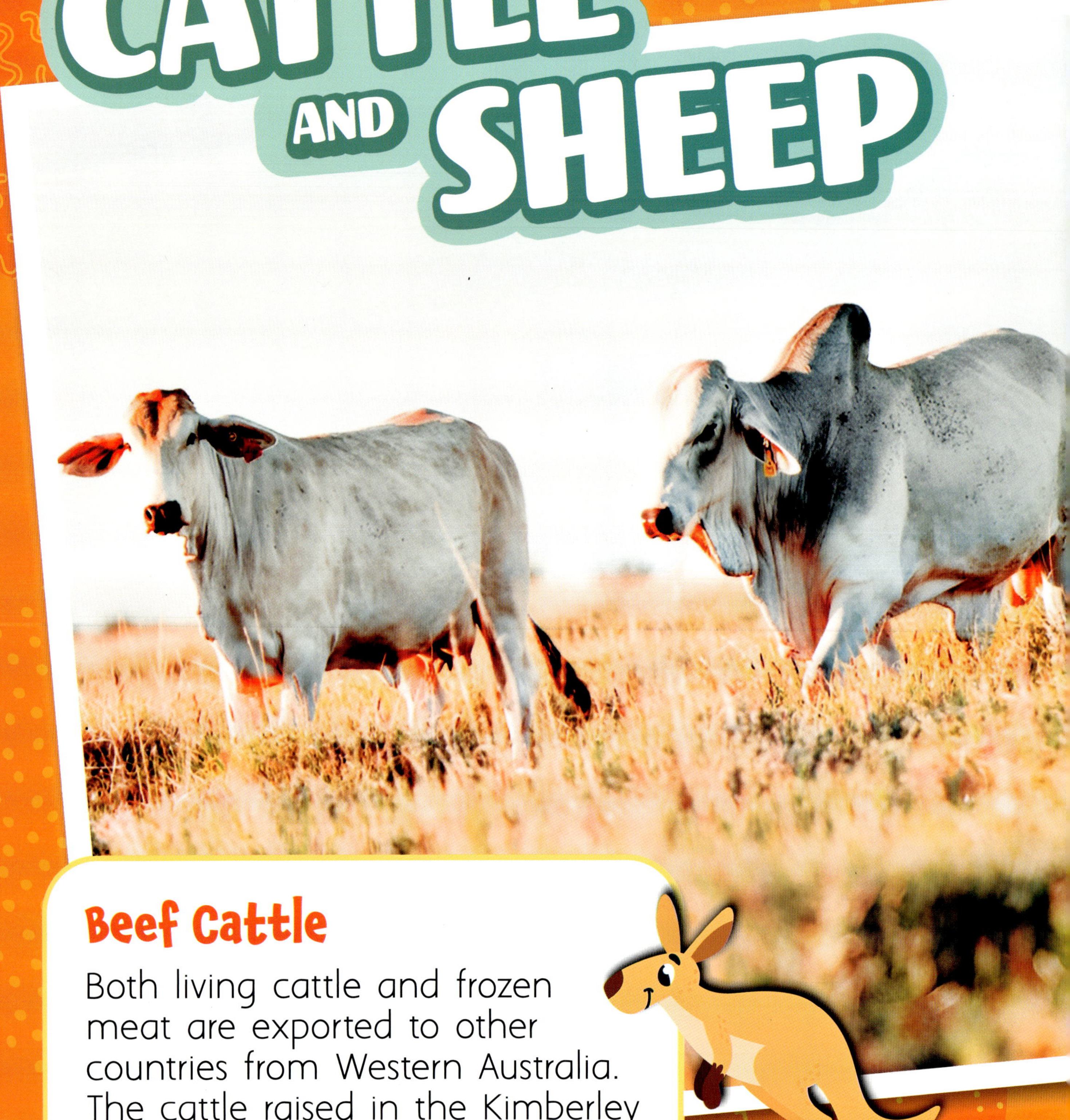

Beef Cattle

Both living cattle and frozen meat are exported to other countries from Western Australia. The cattle raised in the Kimberley are mostly for export.

Sheep

Most of the sheep and lamb meat produced in WA goes overseas.

TRANSPORT IN THE BIGGEST STATE

Eyre Highway

The Eyre Highway is now the main road between WA and the eastern states. It was just a dirt road across the Nullarbor Plain until 1969.

No Roads

The Swan River Settlement in the early 1800s was very isolated. Perth is still one of the most isolated capital cities in the world. There were no roads to it from anywhere in Australia for many years.

Ports

The Port of Fremantle on the Swan River dates from 1829, making it as old as Perth. Most of the imports sent to WA by ship pass through this port.

Port Hedland is the largest bulk port in the world. The iron ore loaded there onto ships mostly goes to China.

Railway

The Trans Australian Railway links WA with the other states. It was finished in 1917.

GOVERNMENT OF WESTERN AUSTRALIA

Western Australia was the last colony to agree to form a Federation and become a state of Australia.

Timeline

1829 - James Stirling was the first Governor of the Swan River Settlement

1890 - WA had its own colonial Parliament with two Houses (or sections)

1899 - Women were allowed to vote in WA

1901 - Federation resulted in WA becoming a state of Australia

Perth Parliament House

The Western Australian Parliament Today

Legislative Council (Upper House) has 36 members.

Legislative Assembly (Lower House) has 59 members.

They meet in Parliament House in Perth.

FLAGS OF WESTERN AUSTRALIA

Australian Aboriginal Flag

The Aboriginal Flag was first flown in 1971. It was designed by elder Harold Thomas in 1970.

What the flag represents:

Yellow Disc	The Sun and yellow ochre
Red	The land
Black	The Aboriginal people of Australia

Western Australian State Flag

The swan on the flag is WA's bird emblem. It is also a reminder of the British settlers who settled beside the Swan River in 1829.

EMBLEMS OF WESTERN AUSTRALIA

Floral Emblem
Red and green kangaroo paw

Animal Emblem
Numbat

Bird Emblem
Black swan

Fossil Emblem
Gogo fish

Marine Emblem
Whale shark

The Coat of Arms

Each part of the Coat of Arms has a meaning:

Kangaroos
Represent the wildlife

Boomerangs
Represent the Indigenous people

Black swan on blue water
Represents the founding of the Swan River Settlement

Crown
Represents the connection with Britain

Flowers
Red and green kangaroo paws are the flower emblem of WA

PEARLS

Pearls used in rings and necklaces come from a special type of oyster that lives in the sea. Most of the world's white South Sea pearls come from the sea off WA near Broome.

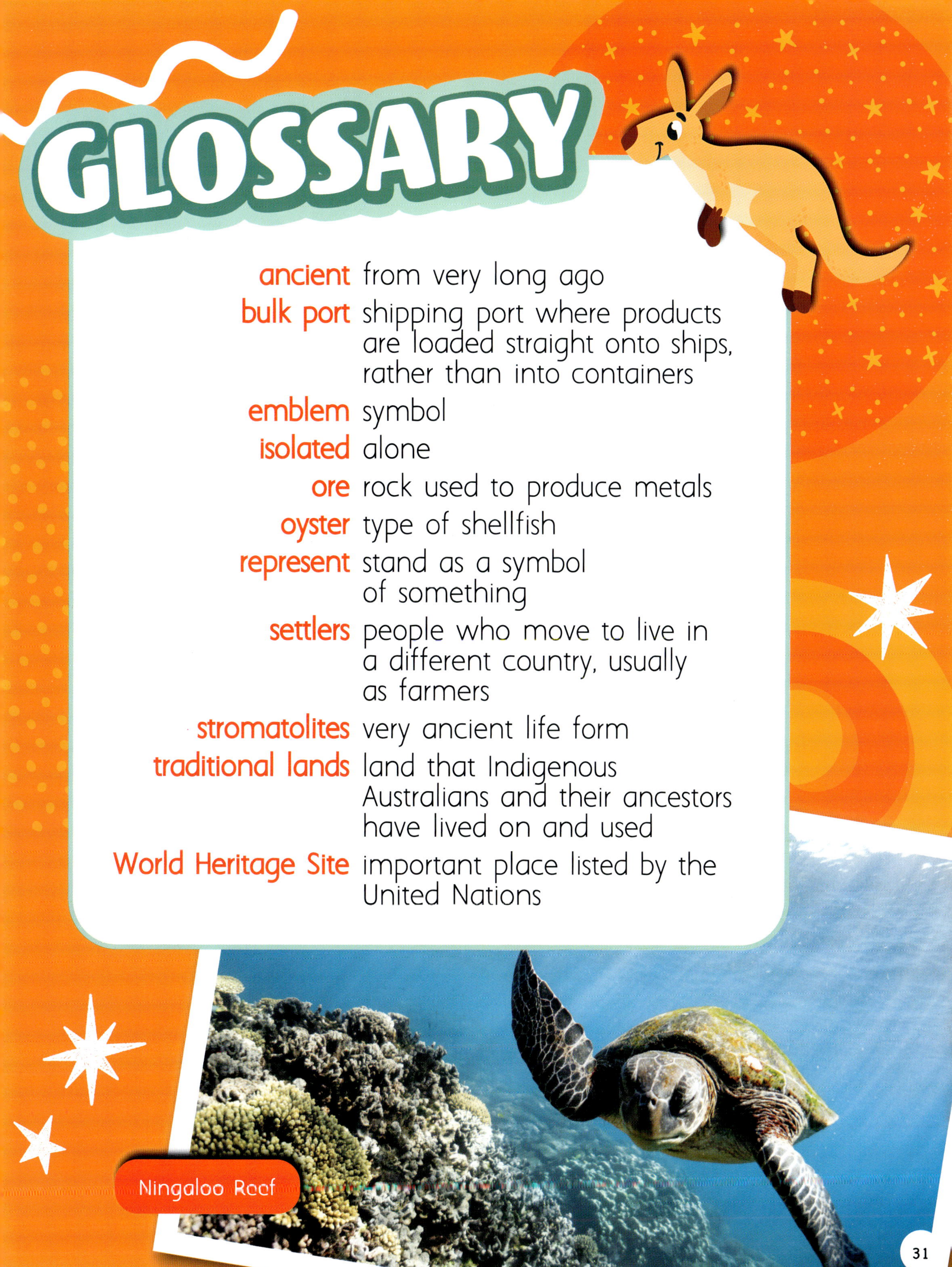

GLOSSARY

ancient from very long ago

bulk port shipping port where products are loaded straight onto ships, rather than into containers

emblem symbol

isolated alone

ore rock used to produce metals

oyster type of shellfish

represent stand as a symbol of something

settlers people who move to live in a different country, usually as farmers

stromatolites very ancient life form

traditional lands land that Indigenous Australians and their ancestors have lived on and used

World Heritage Site important place listed by the United Nations

Ningaloo Reef

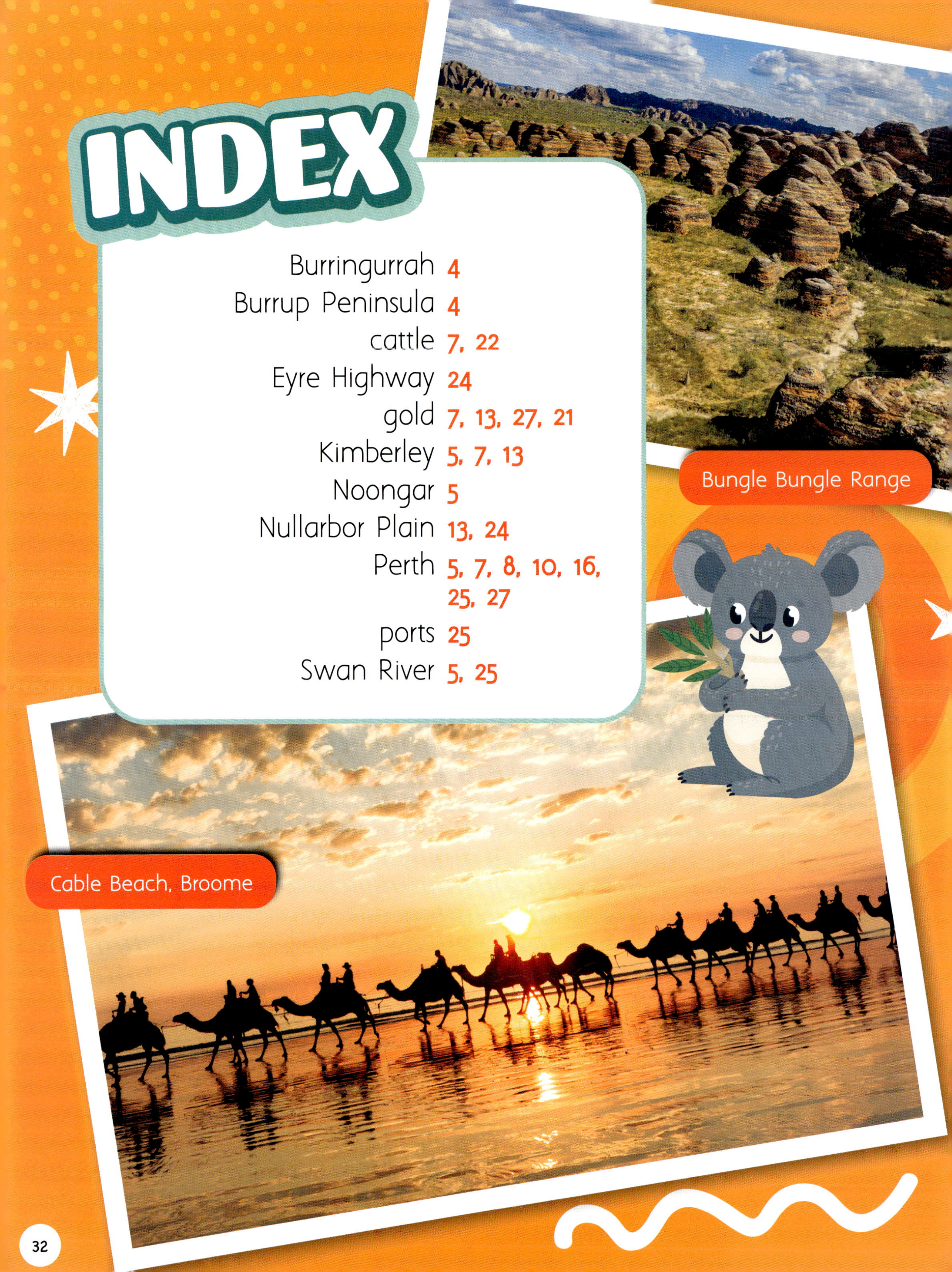

INDEX

Bungle Bungle Range

Cable Beach, Broome

KIDS' GUIDE
TO
AUSTRALIA'S
STATES & TERRITORIES
NT
NORTHERN
TERRITORY
WA
WESTERN
AUSTRALIA